LUSUS

Also by Robert Wells from Carcanet

Selected Poems

Robert Wells

LUSUS

CARCANET

First published in 1999 by
Carcanet Press Limited
4th Floor, Conavon Court
12-16 Blackfriars Street
Manchester M3 5BQ

A CIP catalogue record for this book
is available from the British Library
ISBN 1 85754 382 3

The publisher acknowledges financial assistance
from the Arts Council of England

Set in 10pt Plantin by Bryan Williamson, Frome
Printed and bound in England by SRP Ltd, Exeter

Contents

1

Clearing Ground	9
Bonfire	10
After the Fire	12
Six Emblems	13
Making a Bonfire	16
A Motto	18
Morning	18
Poaching on Exmoor	19
The Fawn	20
Larchtrees	20
'A patch of grass . . .'	21
'The fogbound dusk . . .'	21
'When days open . . .'	22

2

Monte Gennaro Epigrams/One

The Pool	25
The Day	26
The Men who Built the Paths	27
Morning Moments	27
Sunrise	28
'I had no way . . .'	28
Hillside	29
Bathers	29

Monte Gennaro Epigrams/Two

Two Hill-Pools	31
Ruined Shrine	32
Panic	33
The Stream	33
Bather and Horseshoe	34

3

The Last of Summer	37
Summer	41
A Storm	41
Summer Noon	42
Osier Bank	42
Autumn Night	43
Orchid Field	43
The Valley	44
Cascade	44
'Sure in its strength . . .'	45
At Moonrise	45
La Licenza	46

4

No Village Was Too Remote	49
At the Hill-Station	49
In the Meadows	50
Swimmer	50
Night Pieces	51
The Kites	52
Indus	53
Harangue	54
Five Sketches	55
A Likeness	58
Tufan Express	59
The Slope	60
At Old Hall	61
A Robin	61
By the Loire	62
Fishing	62
A Stag at Sea	63
Haymaker	63
Middle Age	64
A Fragment	64

1

Clearing Ground

The hawthorns grew crowded together
In what had been the hill-field.
I had to cut whole thickets away,
Trunk by trunk, before they would fall.

The trees were just in bloom.
I looked up through their dead-seeming
Mesh of twigs at delicate green,
White flowers, open sky –

O need to make things simple by levelling them!

*

I threw the trees, cut into fragments,
On the fire, and watched the green crumple
In an instant in the flame.
                              Later I would find
A twig with flower and leaf still intact
By the circle of the ash.

*

My harshness was the saw's
As it cut through the thicket wall;
My pleasure was the neat blankness
Of cleared ground.
                              Looking across
The shallow curve revealed
Where two slopes met
I would think, 'It was impassable; now
To cross it is as simple as drawing breath.'

I would lie down there,
Spread out my arms and watch the sky.

Bonfire

1

The heaviness of the waste –
Barely to be lifted, a bramble bush on a fork.

Bracken, tons of it, broken down
Year upon year;
                          and trees
So delicate, tapering in the air,
Bulky and gross once fallen.

★

Fire crystallizes about evergreen stems.

On hawthorn bushes the tips of thorns
Ignite and glow.

                          A mesh of birch twigs
Turns black together, some dark smoke
Playing slowly above them amid the flame.

What is the fire?
                It flares or fades
By its own unaccountable law.
There will be the slightest gust of wind
And at this sign it takes,
Making no barrier of
Branches, foliage,
The heaped tangle of thorn
Through which it mounts, pouring upward.

I watch the materials caught
In the rush of heat,
How leaves, stems, twigs
Lose heart, crumble about themselves,
Fold in,
As if the first impulse
Were to withdraw and so escape;

And then, in the very process,
Fly weightlessly apart, upward,
Glowing and crisping,
Turning black, then white, then gone.

                        *

Masterly strength:
                There was a moment,
Once ash and burning charcoal had been amassed
Sufficiently, past which the fire
Would take anything,
Break it of its nature,
Melt it towards itself
– A shape become indistinguishable
In the soft white-red circle.

After the Fire

Stunting shade,
The leaning back towards light;

The wind's shape in the coomb, bending
The tops of larches over, so that they lie
Along the bank of its current
Like sand at a stream's edge;

A hard winter, a burgeoning summer,
A storm, a snowfall –
The evidence in cut wood-rings, torn-off boughs;

A sycamore trunk stripped of its bark by squirrels,
The shredded patch
Where a stag rubbed its itching antlers in spring;

A main-shoot bitten short;

Also like sand the fluted pattern,
Graceful and smooth,
Where for years one branch has blown against another:

Small disparatenesses, the thousand accidents,
All gone to ash.

Six Emblems

1   *'From the felled trunk . . .'*

From the felled trunk the bark
Has rotted away, its wood
Worn into a fibred relief;

Grey-white the scars where branches
Splintered, shrunken the bracken
Which covered it in spring;

Years since the severed life
Died out. What life it has now
Is from the winter sun.

2   *'The sea's blue at dusk . . .'*

The sea's blue at dusk, tiled with waves,
Glazed by the mist,
Deepens.

Across it from the steep-edged coomb
A beech-trunk lifts,
Pale in the drying wind.

3 *'Sun opening the coomb . . .'*

Sun opening the coomb
In the morning
Moves down the side and curves out anew
The gentle incline of its lap,

Like a human goodwill
Illuminating the mind
That dwelt winterlong in shade
As though the shade were life,

And reaches
With a sense of warm discovery
Over budded trees,
Bent bracken, brittle leaf.

4 *'The sapwood rots . . .'*

The sapwood rots;
But where they lie embedded

The hard little cores of broken twigs
Stay sharp.

5   *'Day overcast . . .'*

Day overcast:
A patch of intenser brightness

Folds itself away amid the atmosphere,
Shedding light on the sea –

★

Clarity that, unable to attain
Full sway,

(Some flaw of will preventing it,
Some loss of heart)

Withdraws, prefers to fade,
Leaving only its shadow in the mind.

6   *'Spermatozoa of flame . . .'*

Spermatozoa of flame
Seed the dark, curling
Long momentary tails.

The fire flares at ease –
Could not burn harder
Or be more sheerly itself.

Making a Bonfire

At first I cut carefully what I put on the fire
And lay it carefully,
Twigs, leaves, only a log or two,
So that it won't burn hollow;
Then as heat starts to hold
And the fire is more than a burst of flame –
Has accumulated and springs
From a core of burning ash –

No need to cut up much what I throw on;
It will take branches whole.
The lively flame reaches and plays
Long about the bent and straight, feeling
Through the tangle with its subtle touch
And roaring when it takes.

★

So when the senses
Are kindled, I think, feed them with self –
Slowly at first,
Twigs, leaves, logs,
Cut small, laid carefully;
Then, when flames reach
(What is the flame?)
From the burning fall of ash
(What is the ash?)
Throw on whole branches, dragging them downhill,
One on another, those you need to be rid of,
To clear the ground
For planting, or so that you can walk easily
At least –
Let the flame take them
And melt them unaccountably
In its own way.

Don't let the fire burn hollow,
The branches subdue the flame,
Seared so that they blacken the hands
And the hands the face –
A smoking crisscross of sapwood;
And no enlivening blaze
Hurries you to work, to find more
Before what is there is consumed.

★

The ash sifts and settles,
The fire burns down
In a circle.
                    What is left at the sides –
Pull it away, cut by the flare's extent,
Dried now, quick to draw the flame;
Throw it on; and again
Till nothing is left:

A white-red circle
Bold to the eye when dark falls
Across the cleared hillside.

A Motto

My eyes to the land
My skin to the air

My thirst to water
My memory to fire

Morning

Like mist from water
Sleep steals from the body

Which is discovered
Anew, standing on earth,

The hours before it
As red pales from the sky.

Poaching on Exmoor

In the instant of the shot
The stag raised its head
So that the bullet passed too low,
Through the neck;
And cramming all its anger
Into this moment of offence
It turned and charged at random,
Not marking what had broken the silence
Or brought this sudden pain
From the gentle woodland.

But at once anger dwindled
To an instinct for escape
So that after a few bounds
It veered off into the thicket.
Its legs had not yet learnt
That all its strength was gone,
That the quick circuit
Of its life was broken;
Till in mid-bound
They lost themselves, failed to lift.

It lay filling the coppice
With the rank smell of its maleness,
Brown mane thick at the neck,
Legs tapering and darkening
To black hooves.
    Stepping from the trees
They came to get it with ropes,
And searched the ground but in vain
For a missing antler
Broken off in the flight.

The Fawn

Starting, clumsy and graceful,
From the clumps of bracken at my feet

A fawn tumbles downhill –
Then gathers itself away into the thicket.

Larchtrees

Sun catches the larchtrees
First thing in the morning,
Colouring their trunks
As if with the warmth of rested limbs.

I can hear the owls from them
Last thing at night,
Sending out long calls
Muffled like the beams of light in fog.

'A patch of grass ...'

A patch of grass on scree.
How could it have taken root there?
I lift the stone aside –

Crusting the surface
A pinch of soil, light and dry,
Which wind blows from my fingers.

'The fogbound dusk ...'

The fogbound dusk thickens to rain.
I notice amid the gorse verge

A glowworm's green shine,
And stoop there, fingering the grass aside.

'When days open ...'

When days open and air softens
And sun spills over the sides of hills
That had lain in shade,

Shall body and heart resist?
What else was winter
But a grindstone against which they were set?

Sparks rushed, brittle and heatless,
Against unfeeling hands.
The axe was lifted away, made sharply bright.

Now the birds' undertone
In the morning,
Delighted, sensual, pure –

What is this but the body's ease,
Waking satisfied
And grateful for its dream?

2

Monte Gennaro Epigrams / One

'the custom'd hill'

The Pool

1

What can the water be, other than itself?
I thought it was a fate gathered from the hills,

From each grey cranny, each hollow of moist air,
To glisten on your shoulders, your narrow chest;

And I imagined how you would turn in sleep
In the dark barn as the dream took hold of you,

Its weight and plenty bearing your body down –
A wish disguised, a knowledge not to be kept.

2

The land took everything that was there to take.
What remained was what was unpossessible:

Servitude's counterpart, a hidden freedom
Ghosting your gestures, bringing you to the pool

To learn its own existence over again –
Your weightless body finding in the water

A different poise, the water as it clothed you
Startled alive to its cold buoyant plenty.

The Day

1

Slow climb through darkness to the upland pasture,
Gathering the cattle, driving them to water,

Then down again as sunrise touches the peaks –
Each moment brings its patience. But first this pause:

In the low barn you take an egg from the straw,
Pierce it with a matchstick, stir it, suck it down.

The stars are sharp still, the mountain-ridge seems near.
Freed of its chain your dog whimpers to be off.

2

At nightfall a cold gust shakes down walnut leaves
On the gravel of the roadside as you pass.

Open it for me, the day which your voice holds –
No scared acknowledgement but a full greeting,

Young and clear-spoken, that cherishes its vowels;
Ancient exchange, trace of the hidden city

Whose derelict ways are there to follow still,
Your steps treading back the bramble and the broom.

The Men who Built the Paths

Their shouts bounced off the cliffs, they drank at the springs;
Like flesh from bones they have melted from the land.

They are still with you, the men who built the paths –
You rest in their given unremembered strength.

Morning Moments

1

Trees start to break from darkness and waternoise.
Low mist cobwebs the valley. You look across

To the hidden meadow where your horses graze,
The dew-charged air pricking at your face and hands.

2

Early light. The heavy figtree by the path,
And your word of greeting from the dew-soaked field

Like fruit that is ripe but chilled by the night air,
Concealing something of its taste from the mouth.

Sunrise

Your face still blurred with youth; and the valley-floor
A space that lightens from black through grey to white –

Meadows and stables, riverbed, walls, trees, paths,
Hidden, half-hidden, as the mist thins and shines.

'I had no way . . .'

I had no way of desiring you except
That you should be there, standing under the vines

In the grey of morning, work not yet begun.
I thought that you belonged with the early light,

Calm, uninsistent. But when the sun came up,
Edging above the hill-crest, blackening the hill,

The liveliness hidden in you, quick and sharp,
Made you one with the first beams needling the air.

Hillside

I enter derelict barns, twist myself round
The trunks of broken trees, follow unused paths,

Stand on the sunny ridge where the cliff falls sheer
And on the moss-grown scree at its shadowed base.

I wake past midnight with the moon full on me,
Lighting a musty emptiness in my head,

And walk, as if fated, into the dark air
To take my station against the hill's black edge.

Bathers

Seen from a distance, touches of brown through haze:
They wait on the concrete shelf above the pool,

Unwilling to leave; though, with the afternoon,
The further hill-ridge turns brittle, shadowy.

Storm will involve them as it sweeps the valley
– A premonitory gust through willow scrub,

So that they shiver; then the first scattered drops,
Heavy and sudden, pockmarking the warm dust.

Monte Gennaro Epigrams / Two

Two Hill-Pools

1

The noise of water, shutting out other sounds,
Has drawn him down from the hill-path to the pool.

A tense complicity brings him here to bathe.
His body is never more itself than now,

All feeling gone except for the buffetting
Cascade, a dissolving screen across his eyes.

What is it that he is left with? What survives
The torrent's numbing onrush and pulls him clear?

2

Again to meet it. Turning aside at dusk
Where path and streambed cross, to follow the stream.

Waylaid by an old temptation or belief,
He stumbles along the deepening corridor

To find – what is it? – something live but other,
And his body's recognition startles him.

The wide ripples push out from a thin cascade,
Green, white, pale. A colour that he cannot name.

Ruined Shrine

1

Cliff-rooted oak coppice, slopes of thorny brush,
Thick forest, sudden lawns close-cropped and dewy,

Heavy curtainings of lime-encrusted moss
– As if a city were overrun with green.

Here the dead keep him company; their language
His to recover, the good sense of the paths.

Where the track is overgrown he feels it still,
A level, a direction, beneath his tread.

2

A grassy cattle-pen on the hill's shoulder,
Some tumbled blocks lying among broom and bracken

Strewn down the slope. Surface by weathered surface
He searches out their vestiges of design,

Like clues to a language that might be reclaimed,
In a portion of its sense, from some few words –

A curved fragment of cornice, a grey rosette
Curling its petals for the finger to trace.

Panic

Swift sky, snow-crusted boulders, brown oak-coppice,
Dry leaves waiting dislodgement. Then he heard it,

Out of the air beside him a long-drawn groan
As if a body were turning from its wound –

What wound? In terror he plunged away and down
Till he found a path. There was a bridge below,

Its arch of smoothed stones evidencing a life
Perfectly fitted. And yet such room for fear.

The Stream

Pouring of water through the night, through the year,
The last sound before sleep, the first on waking;

Transparent path, almost overgrown beside
The trodden path's embankment of earth and stone;

Clear-bodied wholeness at the field's edge, logic
Finding out the lowest place, the easiest way;

An elemental beside a human sense,
Where he kneels to drink, to paint his skin with cold.

Bather and Horseshoe

1

Spring weather; days of alternate storm and sun.
Pausing at the bridge, he looks aside to where

The torrent spills from a concrete breakwater
To flood a hollow scooped in the bed below;

And sees – emblem of a pristine completeness –
A bather standing among the willow scrub,

Gentle and exact, feet curded with the dust,
Letting air dry him; who turns, then turns away.

2

Burst walls, rough fields, the dilapidated path:
Among loose stones the fragment of a horseshoe

Scraped thin and bright at the edge, one rusted nail
Adhering still. Picking it up, he studies

The fine pattern of scratches on its surface
As if some meaning which he could not construe

Were to be found engraved in the worn metal;
And thinks again of the figure by the pool.

3

The Last of Summer

1

What shall I find in fields running to waste?
      How fix the care
That stirs in me, aimless as autumn air –
Without an object but the sweet white taste

Of hazelnuts, or blackberries, the last few?
      And then to sleep
For half the morning, shepherd without sheep,
Stretched where the early sun has dried the dew

And in some nook its delicate warmth is held.
      The thoughts that I
Tried to brush off as daydream, fantasy,
Destructive of the nature I had willed –

I let these in; with them, the recollection
      Of how my shame
Was shot with beams, withdrew till it became
A mutual joke, a part of shared affection.

Enigma's place, the hollow among boulders –
        The old demand
Which drew me back repeatedly to stand
Where the stream broke about my head and shoulders

In stifling plenty; the cold shock, the sense
        Of boundaries
Reached and restored, the supervening ease;
– Proofs of a kinship between elements,

The world's, my body's, which importunately
        Required its due:
All these composed a rite supplanted now
By a stronger claim, a nearer memory.

Needless for me to look for what will come
        Without a greeting
In its own time. Time enough, at that meeting,
To crouch beneath the onrush, battered, numb.

3

Chirr of cicadas, the always-running stream,
        The heat-filled day –
As far as the land reached, these reached away.
Each day labour would make me one with them.

Existence through effacement! Anything less
        Seemed less than life
To me. I felt the pull of the world, as if
The senses were a sum of consciousness

Claiming me fully. What they could not gather
        Into their trance –
The faults and griefs – was mere inconsequence,
Theirs the whole story cancelling every other

Without a hearing. Yet the whole story none,
        Or what was told
By water in its course, will-less and cold;
By spots of sweat fading on sunwarmed stone.

4

Squat mounds of bramble cast their shade,
      Marked out with dew,
Across low turf. The track's brown curlicue
Climbs to thyme-scented slope and broomy glade.

Hazel and blackthorn skirt the stream –
      A trickle still,
Running in its grey cranny from pool to pool.
Between dry stalks spider-threads drift and gleam.

The meadow in the slanting sun
      Shows as it was,
But changed invisibly to leavetaking's place,
The mastering fullness of the summer gone.

I'm claimed by a gentler revery,
      A kinder embrace.
Love's smile, which can't be kept out of the face,
Is what I come from and what waits for me.

Summer

The cold will-less muscle
Of water pushes at my hand.

The grass moves in the sun,
A floating pell-mell of shadow.

A Storm

A meadow afloat with white campion, wild parsley;
The hill-ridges grey now with sunlit shadow –

What to do with this beauty except stay for it?
But I up and run from the lightning's pale flare.

Summer Noon

1

Theatre of hills –
An audience of cicadas
Applauding summer.

2

The blood starting
In a fine column
From the mule's flank
– A horsefly bite.

3

Hung in a treefork,
The viper's drying carcase
Eaten out by ants.

Osier Bank

Under willow bushes
A dewy hollow –
The air still fresh at noon.

Autumn Night

1

One star through the cloud
That drifts more thickly in. Far off,
A chained dog moans.

2

A moonless darkness –
Water and air no longer
Extend their welcome.

3

I sleep unwashed and warm,
Sheathed in the honey smell
Of hay from the stack.

Orchid Field

Greenwings – purple lamps
Making their own light
In the shadow of a briar.

The Valley

The barrier through which the body has to fight
Is the body, yours and the world's. Time and again

It emerges beyond itself, transfigured, lightened,
Yet at a loss; as when, climbing past a ridge,

You come out above the head of a trackless valley
– Yours to gaze over, pleasant in the morning sun –

And, caught in the promise of its light and shadow,
Stand with it at your feet but do not go down there.

Cascade

Beneath the noise
(Like rocks knocking together)
Of water as it plunges –

A hum, a thin stridency,
As if a trapped column of air
Shook in fine vibration.

'Sure in its strength ...'

Sure in its strength the body drew
Stones with deliberateness to the chest,
With accuracy spaded the earth into
The panniers slung over the mule.
                                    There was

Surely a mood of real content
When dusk unfocussed the air's smoky glass
And made the olives plumes of a grey mist
And my skin was grey with sacks of cement.

At Moonrise

Youth's good was its own body
Which did not fail.
At moonrise I would dive naked
Into the pool,

Splinter the beams, surface,
Watch them regather.
Self-knowledge was no more
Than the touch of water.

La Licenza

You withdraw further, are lost to the mind's eye,
Sinking away into the path, the hillside,
The patch of dusty ground among willow scrub
By the valley-pool; and these too disappear
Like being young, like the lively contentment
That keeps its energy . . . my admiration
Gone with the scene where it had play, the river
No longer batheable, the paths repossessed
By thorns, by rockfalls. Who would need to pass there?
An aged used landscape! Let the process of loss
Go unrecorded. This is – this was – the place
Where expectation took on its clearest shape
And promise was most substantial, breathed alike
In the dew-shedding air of early morning,
Carrier of greetings; in the heat-crammed noon;
The passivity of dusk, at summer's end
Undermined by gusts of wind and colder dark.

4

No Village Was Too Remote
the Iran-Iraq War

The roadside soft with dust, the threadbare hills,
The teahouse with its incongruous velvet couch,
The felt-capped boy stopping with his goats to stare:
Dusk drew these together in a frail coherence
As the moon rose, strengthening through deep-blue air.

In that dry numinous light, it seemed, the country
Lay changelessly far off, and the childish face
Unreachably open between domed cap and coat.
I count the years now to reckon the herdboy's age,
And guess the sequel. No village was too remote.

At the Hill-Station

A room at the hill-station, fireless, bare.
No view. The hills are lost in mist-clogged air.

Plenty of space, though, to walk up and down
Thinking of unfilled spaces of my own.

49

In the Meadows

A landing-place, stone coping heaved by roots,
Steps down to water, two rustless iron rings:
Finding these, I imagined a river-journey
From the city to a palace outside the walls.

Cattle range in deep grass, trample the shade –
No building more than a barn ever stood here.
But clear in my mind as when I was a boy
The palace's shape and the courtesies it housed.

Swimmer

Swimming upriver between tree-walled banks
Through hidden reaches scummed with dust and blossom,

I felt the water's plenty, its slow movement –
A largesse I need never cease to give from.

Night Pieces

1

You have freed me from the will's aghast attempt
To reach beyond itself, my lonely effort
On the unkempt hillside, in the empty house.

We move through pleasure, beneficent and shared,
Toward a necessity that neither hastens
Nor interrupts our voluntary approach.

What scenes come back, once that necessity
Is touched and we lie separately, cast loose
In the enormous dark! This room becomes

The world in which we have travelled and seen sights.
Here memory is gathered into consequence,
Taken from chance and made a part of us.

2

Your sanity was my presence.
I lie here, safe, alone
And share your sleeplessness –

Imagining how the beasts,
Made tame by sympathy,
Range round you in the desert.

The Kites

On Parliament Hill that grey-skied afternoon
We watched the kites being flown. Out over the Heath
Each frail construction hung as if alone,
And single motionless figures stood beneath.
Which figure held which string could not be guessed.
The kites were anonymous and unpossessed.

It would not be like this, you said, at home.
There a family crest would decorate each kite,
And the sky would offer scarcely any room
As each strained to outride the other's height,
Tangling and intercepting in mock battle
Amid the confusion of the festival.

We stared at the chilly steadfast English view.
I thought of the need for open space, cold air,
Unsociably assuaged in me; while you
Were lost in your memory of India.
We both found unfamiliar company,
I in your crowded, you in my empty sky.

Indus

The threadbare hand-me-down
of empire, your notion of the 'gentleman'
hid a code unsearchably
more ancient. Lying beside you

I reached out past our attic room
to a low flat-roofed mansion,
straw-rough walls, a bed,
a body that moves and moans –

remote scene of pleasure
conjured from a valley-town
whose bricks had melted back to earth
before any named event.

Harangue

You bowed before
the well-appointed certainties
in my rhetoric of reproach,
and listened to the sound

with the attention due
to an unshareable creed,
its heavy dictates
lost on your unbelief.

What you heard rather
was a conqueror's innocence,
comic and enviable,
lending me crass strength

– a notional safety
in which, through me, you might rest,
taking for solid ground
the black space open beneath you.

Five Sketches

1

'You must realize that I am very superficial.
I have been brought up that way – to talk
About this and that.
                   This poet oh yes,
This general oh yes.
                     Five minutes' conversation.'

★

I exhorted you to read 'about Indian history',
Talked of 'your culture'
– 'You should root yourself more firmly. . . .'

Innocent words. You smiled at my hectoring,

And preferred the chat of the moment, the dance-floor;
To glide, leaving no wake;
                   for fixity
(You taught me how to teach you)
To crouch, trapped fugitive,
In a submission which made you gasp and moan.

2

Your fantasy of annihilation
Was a joke to me. But when the girl's straw hat
Blew down between live rails
You jumped from the platform to fetch it
As if your life
                      weighed as lightly as the hat –
And handed it back, grinning,
Moments before the train hurtled through.

Was it this brave carelessness
Put paid to the attempt
To make an accountant of you?
                                        Certainly
You were no 'economist of your person'.

3

The pearl in the wine, my 'right gipsy'!

– And you kissing away
My Roman shock
                      at the improvidence.

4

A spring of failed exams, of tears;
A summer of 'could-be's', wishful hopes
While you 'sung and hopped
In meadows green' –

'And now green ice':
                    the bureaucrat's
Sleights matching yours, his guarded voice
And sly relish for the order of things;
Your passport returned, visa unrenewed,
Invalid,
          having been kept all year.

5

Tears – suddenly at the barrier
As we embraced, then uselessly
On the Terminal roof
As, unclean with fatigue, I watched
Your plane take off,
                    grow small,
Its steep thrust vanish in cloud;

And the thought
That for someone landing today
The story now beginning

Was the same story
                    over again.

A Likeness

Portrait Coins
of the Greco-Indian Kings:
turning the pages
I come upon a face
– your double's, clear
as in a photograph,
stamped in ancient silver:
a medallion head
from Taxila, full-lipped,
eyes deepset and large,
a hard expression
on features softly rounded
where disillusion
and suspicions amongst thoughts
combine oddly and cruelly
with generous feeling –
the trustful candour
of childhood still evident
in its opposite;
I recognize this
in him – this, and something too
of division suffered and relished,
a hybrid culture:
beneath the classic forms,
the inscription,
the moulding of the bust,
a different presence,
landlocked, indigenous,
swaying his look;
a further reach
of belonging than the Greek
(which was still his)
– Athena Promachos
from remote Pella
fighting on the reverse
but vainly . . .
and the Kharoshti
legend around.

Tufan Express

Washed-out brightness
of the saris
of field-working women;

the white dome glimpsed,
majestically elaborate,
above avenues of green;

a peacock agilely
managing its burden
of tailfeathers as it scuttles
across embankment and ditch:

what can these avail?

– sudden magnificence
ineffectual against
the meagre repetition
of plains, roads, hills.

The Slope

Love's risky dealing –
I think of the ploughman
who ploughs too steep
or miscalculates the slope.

The machine goes over
suddenly (he must leap
clear or be crushed) –
over and over, buckling,

breaking into pieces,
till caught against the torn
bark of a tree
at the coomb's base

and left there,
beyond retrieval, rust
starting to discolour
the bared wood of the trunk.

At Old Hall

for Peter Scupham

Shepherds still follow their sheep where Hesiod
Once met the Muses stepping out of the mist.

(I conjure the place: wooded slopes and a path,
Hammocks of meadow slung between rocky crests.)

Are they to be met, too, in our lowland fields,
By our slow rivers, the Waveney or the Loire?

Down here they need a lower roof than the sky.
Where should they shelter but in your open house?

A Robin

Geldeston Marshes

Plumping your feathers you come close for company,
Peck at the bark of a twig, at a grain in mud.

I notice how pale it is, the grey patch between
The rust-colour of the breast, the brown of the wing.

Then you make off through a fallen willow's tangle
– Out across the striped alternation of ripples.

Leant against an ivied trunk, I stare at the reeds
That stand up, dry and faded, from black reflections.

By the Loire

1

Grey heron –
Its shadow in the water
More visible than itself.

2

A kingfisher
– Or a torn scrap
Of turquoise litter
Snagged on a branch?

3

Ragged phoenix –
The cormorant, wings held open,
On its stone-island.

Fishing

His body is a shell
held
to what it is
in him
that listens.

A Stag at Sea
(forced out by the hounds)

Head back in the crisp waves and antlers back,
The winter mane sea-darkened at its neck,
A fated creature, never out of view,
Treads water in the empty field of blue.

Haymaker

Work is finished. He stands in the dark field,
Cleared of its bales, the last trailer gone in.

A delusive freshness reaches through his body
As if moonrise were the sign for him to begin.

Middle Age

The temples, lakes and islands; rooms and roads:
When we go wandering, soon there's too much
To gather into consequence. Our touch
Has brushed too many stones; too many gods
Have played the host to us and had their claim
Shrugged off. Old pockets, worn-out wallets keep
The bills and tickets. In a drawer, a heap
Of shells recalls a place, perhaps a name.

Youth's body, like a broken statue, lies
Deep-buried with the meaning that it gave.
We cast about for something we can save
By which to save ourselves; more blank than wise
For all the miles that brought us to this ground,
Still ignorant of where value can be found.

A Fragment
Paestum

O sun at morning on the ruined town.
O parting, no abasement in farewell.

O light upon the temple's golden stone
Cut by the salt-edged air, a burning shell.